Contents

Words in **bold** can be found in the glossary on page 28.

Call the Coastguard!

All kinds of **emergencies** can happen near the coast. Swimmers may be swept out to sea. A boat could be in trouble. If you see an emergency near the coast, call 999. Ask for the Coastguard. »

If you are worried about a boat or a swimmer near the coast, call the Coastguard.

>> The Coastguard contacts the service that can help. It might be the **Navy**, air ambulance or the Coastguard cliff rescue team.

If the emergency is at sea, the Coastguard may call the RNLI. This is the Royal National Lifeboat Institution.

The Coastguard may need to call out its helicopter. Here, the Coastguard and the RNLI are practising their rescue skills.

The RNLI lifeboat team

Most people who work for the RNLI are volunteers – they are not paid. »

Here are some members of Brighton RNLI. All of this team are volunteers.

» There are different jobs. The lifeboat manager decides when to launch a lifeboat. **Shore helpers** launch the lifeboat. The lifeboat crew go out on the lifeboat to rescue people. »

Lifeboats are kept in a boathouse by the water.

>> Some RNLI volunteers give out free safety advice to people who have boats.

At the boathouse, RNLI **mechanics** make sure that the lifeboats are kept in good order.

The mechanic at Shoreham RNLI checks a lifeboat engine.

The lifeboats

There are two kinds of lifeboat – inshore and all-weather. The inshore lifeboat is open. It travels up to 80 kilometres from the shore. It can rescue people near rocks or cliffs. Up to 20 people can fit on it! »

The Atlantic 75 inshore lifeboat

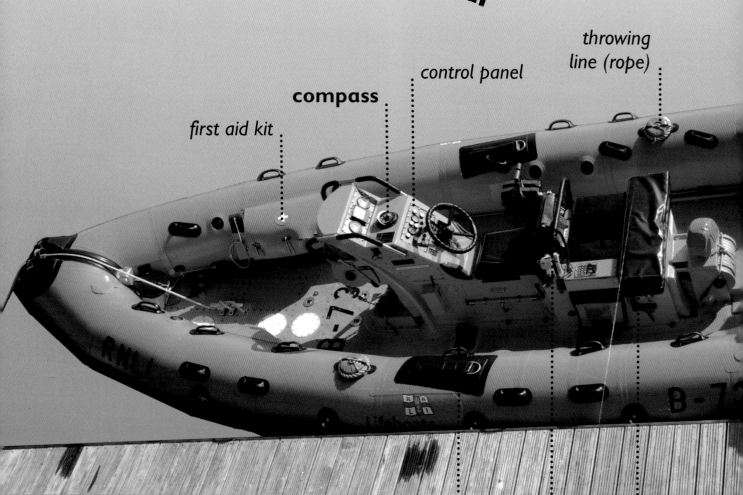

first aid kit

compass

control panel

throwing line (rope)

hand hold

radio speaker

equipme store

>> The all-weather lifeboat can rescue people up to 180 kilometres from the coast. It can carry up to 100 people.

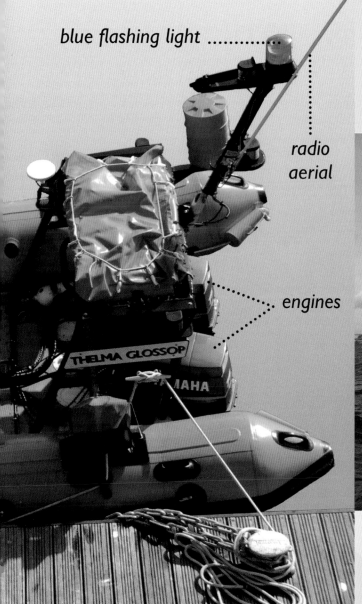

blue flashing light ....

radio aerial

engines

THELMA GLOSSOP

YAMAHA

47-040

The all-weather lifeboat can be used even in huge storms. If it turns over in the water, it rolls back the right way up.

Ready to go

The Coastguard takes the 999 call. If someone is in trouble at sea, the Coastguard calls the RNLI lifeboat manager. The lifeboat manager pages the crew. When the **pager** goes off, it's very loud!

The crew members stop what they are doing and rush to the lifeboat station. They arrive in just five minutes and put on their kit. »

The crew can change into their kit in seconds.

The inshore lifeboat kit

safety helmet

dry suit

life jacket

safety hook

reflective strips

gloves

note pad

boots with steel toe cap and sole

Launching the lifeboat

The lifeboat crew make their way to the lifeboat as quickly as possible. »

The crew run to the lifeboat.

» Some crew members stay at the station. One person keeps in touch with the lifeboat and other emergency services by radio. Others are on **standby**. They may need to help with a beach search. »

The Brighton inshore lifeboat launches from a floating boathouse.

» It's time to launch! An inshore lifeboat may be launched using a tractor and **trailer**. Sometimes, a crane, **floating boathouse** or **slipway** is used. The all-weather lifeboat may already be in the water or go down a slipway.

This all-weather lifeboat zooms down the slipway. It enters the water with a big splash!

Lifeboat equipment

The lifeboat is packed with life-saving equipment. »

compass to find out the direction

floating throw bag with line (rope) to throw to a person who cannot be reached

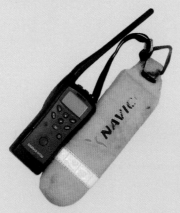

radio with float bag

searchlight to use in the dark

bolt croppers to cut down the wires that support the mast of a boat, to rescue the crew

air horn

white **flare** to give light for searching

rope for **towing** *another boat*

first aid *kit*

safety harness to clip people on to the lifeboat in rough weather

torch

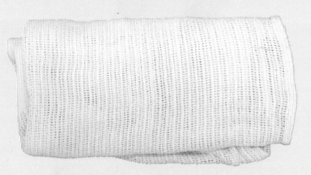

blanket to warm up survivors

resuscitation *bag with* **oxygen cylinder**

A crew member uses an air horn. When the crew are towing a boat, it warns other boats to keep out of the way.

To the rescue!

People can be in trouble at sea in all weathers. In rough weather, accidents are more likely. It is dangerous for the lifeboat crew, too. There may be high winds, big waves and pouring rain. Strong **currents** pull the boat. »

Sometimes, a boat runs out of fuel or a crew member falls ill. Here, the lifeboat has been called out to a sailing boat.

Some people in kayaks have gone **adrift** in a storm. The lifeboat crew pull the first person on to the all-weather lifeboat.

>> The lifeboat crew understand the **tides**. They know how to **navigate** the boat through stormy seas.

Team work

The RNLI works with other emergency services. It often works with the Coastguard rescue team. The coastguards help people who are lost, trapped or hurt on the coast. Here, coastguards are looking for a missing woman. »

The Shoreham coastguards carry searchlights and hold a rope to make sure they stay together in the dark.

>> The coastguards soon find the woman. She has hurt her leg while climbing on some rocks. The coastguards carry her up the beach on a **stretcher**. An ambulance is waiting to take her to hospital.

The coastguards carry first aid equipment and a stretcher with them.

Training the crew

It takes about a year to train as a lifeboat crew member. Trainees learn at the lifeboat station. They also go to courses at the RNLI's college in Poole, Dorset. »

All the lifeboat crew keep up their training. Every week, they take out the lifeboat for training at sea.

>> Lifeboat trainees learn first aid so they can help people who have got into trouble on the water. They also find out how to use the lifeboat and all the equipment on board.

The lifeboat crew practise resuscitation on a dummy.

The crew learn how to navigate the lifeboat.

Learning about the RNLI

Schools and groups such as the Cubs and Brownies can visit the lifeboat station. RNLI volunteers tell them about the RNLI and how to stay safe near water. »

«« A visitor to the lifeboat station sits in the seat of the person who steers the boat.

» The RNLI also runs open days to tell people about its sea rescue service. It is a charity. It needs to raise funds to pay for the lifeboats. People find out about the RNLI and they give money. Then it can carry on its important work.

At an open day, visitors look around the lifeboats and talk to the crew about their work.

Staying safe near water

When you are near water, follow this important advice to keep safe.

Spot the dangers. The water may be very deep. There could be strong currents.

Always go to the beach with other people, not alone.

Find and follow the safety signs and flags. Only swim in the sea where there is a lifeguard.

Emergency? Stick up your hand and shout, or ring 999. »

When you go on a boat, always wear a life jacket. It will help you float if you fall in.

Lifeguards help to keep people safe on the beach. They use **binoculars** to keep an eye on swimmers and **surfers**.

>> If you follow this advice, you can have fun, but stay safe, when you are near the water.

Glossary

adrift
Floating without being controlled by anyone.

binoculars
Special glasses for seeing a long way away.

compass
An instrument for working out the direction.

current
The flow of water in the sea.

dry suit
A suit that keeps out water.

emergencies
Serious situations that happen suddenly and need immediate attention.

equipment
Tools and machines that are designed to do a particular job.

first aid
Emergency treatment given to someone who is sick or injured.

flare
A device that burns to make a bright light.

floating boathouse
A place where a boat is kept. It is not on land, but floats on the water instead.

life jacket
A jacket that helps you to float if you fall in the water.

mechanic
A person who repairs machines.

navigate
To find your way, especially at sea.

Navy
The armed force that fights at sea.

oxygen cylinder
A container with oxygen gas in it.

pager
A device that makes a sound when someone wants to contact you.

resuscitation
Reviving a person who has no signs of life.

shore helpers
People who help to launch the lifeboat.

slipway
A sloping ramp or track

standby
Waiting in case you are needed.

stretcher
A device like a cot for carrying an injured person.

surfer
A person who rides on waves using a board.

tide
The regular rise and fall of the sea level.

towing
Pulling a boat using a rope.

trailer
A truck or a container with wheels that is pulled by another vehicle.

Finding out more

Books

Lifeboat Crew Member by Rebecca Hunter (Cherrytree, 2008)

Rescue at Sea by Clare Oliver (Franklin Watts, 2006)

Websites

HM Coastguard Sea Smart Storytelling in Libraries
http://www.mcga.gov.uk
Search for 'Storytelling'. Contains free pack with stories to teach about sea and beach safety.

RNLI site for young people
http://www.rnli.org.uk/shorething
Has games and activities.

RoSPA Water Safety for Children and Young People
http://www.rospa.com
Search for 'water safety children'. Inclues the water safety code, rescue methods and quiz.

Note to parents and teachers: every effort has been made by the Publishers to ensure that these websites are suitable for children, that they are of the highest educational value, and that they contain no inappropriate or offensive material. However, because of the nature of the Internet, it is impossible to guarantee that the contents of these sites will not be altered. We strongly advise that Internet access is supervised by a responsible adult.

Index